NSOROMA INSTITUTE
22180 Parklawn
Oak Park, MI 48237

LIVING AND WORKING TOGETHER

FAMILIES

BOOK 1

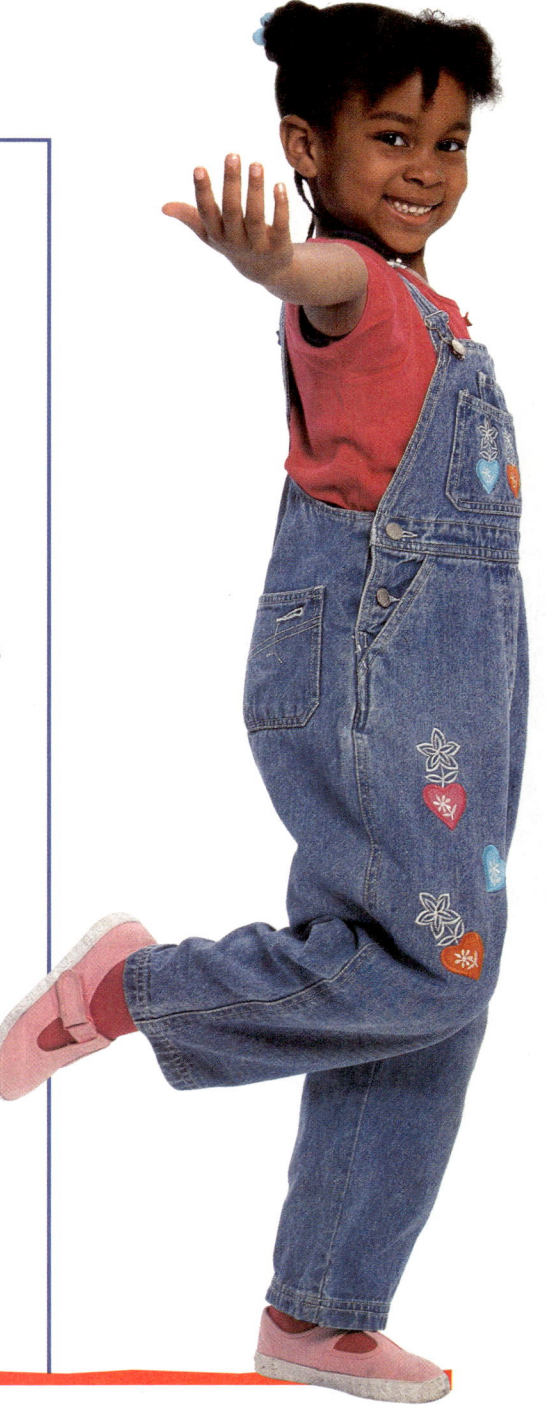

Detroit Public Schools

David Adamany
Chief Executive Officer

Juanita Clay Chambers
Associate Superintendent
Division of Educational Services

Dahia Shabaka
Director
Office of Social Studies

**Published by
Metropolitan Teaching
and Learning Company**

Reginald Powe
President

Juwanda G. Ford
Managing Editor

The Office of Social Studies, under the auspices of the Division of Educational Services, selected a cadre of educators to create early elementary social studies instructional materials. All of the individuals listed in the categories below were or are still teachers or administrators with the Detroit Public Schools.

Senior Author: Dahia Shabaka

Authors: Marva Brown, Barbara Calloway, Janet Fulton, Marie Harris, Annie Mae Holt, Cathy Johnson, Dr. Jonella Mongo, Chaka Nantambu, Cynthia A. Spencer, Dr. Patsy Stewart, Charles W. Summer

Consultant: Cathy Johnson

Project Editor: Dr. Jonella Mongo

Acknowledgments: David Adamany, Chief Executive Officer, Detroit Public Schools; Juanita Clay Chambers, Associate Superintendent, Division of Educational Services, Detroit Public Schools; Ellen Stephens, former Deputy Superintendent, Division of Educational Services, Detroit Public Schools

METROPOLITAN PUBLISHING STAFF

Managing Editor: Juwanda G. Ford

Production: Cheryl Hudson

Design Staff: Virginia Graziano, Charles Yuen

Editorial Staff: Linda Ekblad, Elspeth Leacock, Bruce T. Paddock, Jennifer Rose

Copy Chief: Joyce M. Gaskin

Copyright ©1999 Metropolitan Teaching and Learning Company. Published by Metropolitan Teaching and Learning Company. All rights reserved. No part of this book may be reproduced or utilized in any form or by any means, electronic or mechanical, including photocopying, recording, or by any information storage and retrieval system without permission in writing from the publisher.

For information regarding permission, write to the address below.

Metropolitan Teaching and Learning Company
33 Irving Place
New York, NY 10003

Printed in the United States of America
ISBN: 1-58120-820-0

CONTENTS

vi Your Textbook at a Glance

UNIT 1 We All Have a Family

- 4 **LESSON 1** What Kind of Family Do You Have?
- 8 **LESSON 2** Families Care
- 10 **LESSON 3** Rules Help Families
- 12 **SKILLS** Looking Down
- 14 **LESSON 4** A Family Is a Team
- 18 **SKILLS** Using Maps
- 20 **LESSON 5** Solving Family Problems
- 22 **UNIT 1 REVIEW**

UNIT 2 We Are a Family at School

26	LESSON 1	New Friends
30	SKILLS	Using Map Keys
32	LESSON 2	Our School Family Cares For Us
36	LESSON 3	Home and School Together
40	LESSON 4	Rules At School
44	SKILLS	Finding Directions on a Map
46	LESSON 5	Solving Problems At School
48	SKILLS	Using Charts
50	UNIT 2 REVIEW	

UNIT 3 Two Families Look Back

54	LESSON 1	Our Story: A Chippewa Family
58	LESSON 2	My Family in Africa
62	SKILLS	Finding the Main Idea
64	LESSON 3	My Family in Early America
66	LESSON 4	My Family in Detroit
70	SKILLS	Using Time Lines
72	SKILLS	Reading Photographs
74	UNIT 3 REVIEW	

Reference Section

R2	Atlas, the United States
R4	Atlas, the World
R6	Dictionary of Geography
R8	Picture Glossary
R14	Index

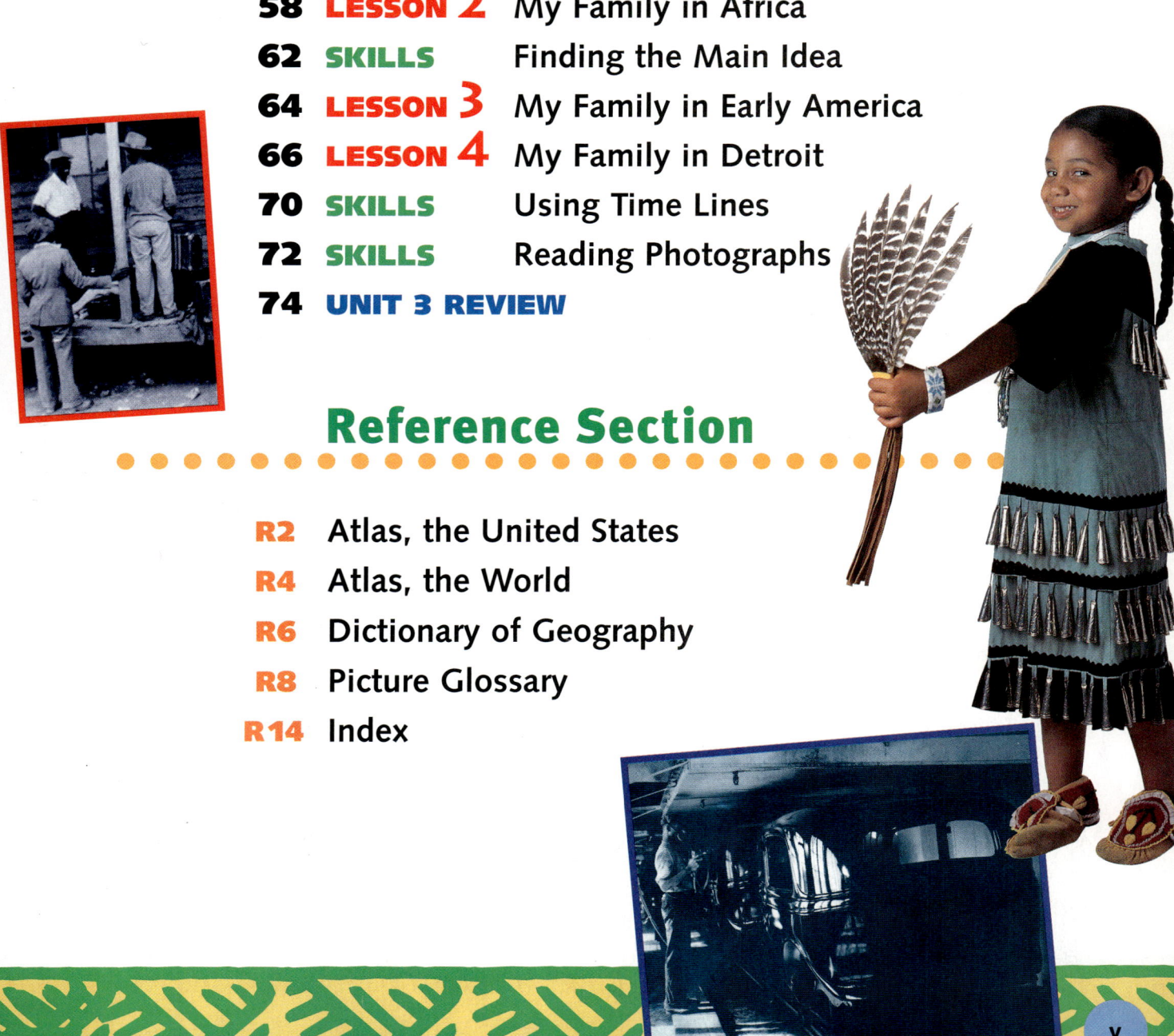

THIS BOOK WAS WRITTEN JUST FOR YOU.

LESSON 1: WHAT KIND OF FAMILY DO YOU HAVE?

Sekou and Kimisha are brother and sister. Their family has four people. Their **family** is the people they live with. Sekou and Kimisha live with their mother and father.

Kevin lives with his grandfather. Grandfather takes good care of Kevin. They talk and eat and play together. Kevin likes his family just the way it is.

There are three units in your book.

LESSON 2: FAMILIES CARE

Families give love. They help us see the good things about ourselves. Maya tells her grandmother about her day at school. Grandmother listens to Maya. This is one way family members show that they care.

Tiffany wants to learn how to swim. Her aunt helps her do things that are new to her. Her family makes time for Tiffany. This is another way that families show that they care.

Who helps you in your family?

Each unit has four to five lessons.

There are skills for you to practice.

A Unit Close and Skills Review help you remember what you have learned.

Unit 1

WE ALL HAVE A FAMILY

Our families are the people we live with. Families are alike in some ways. They are different in some ways, too.

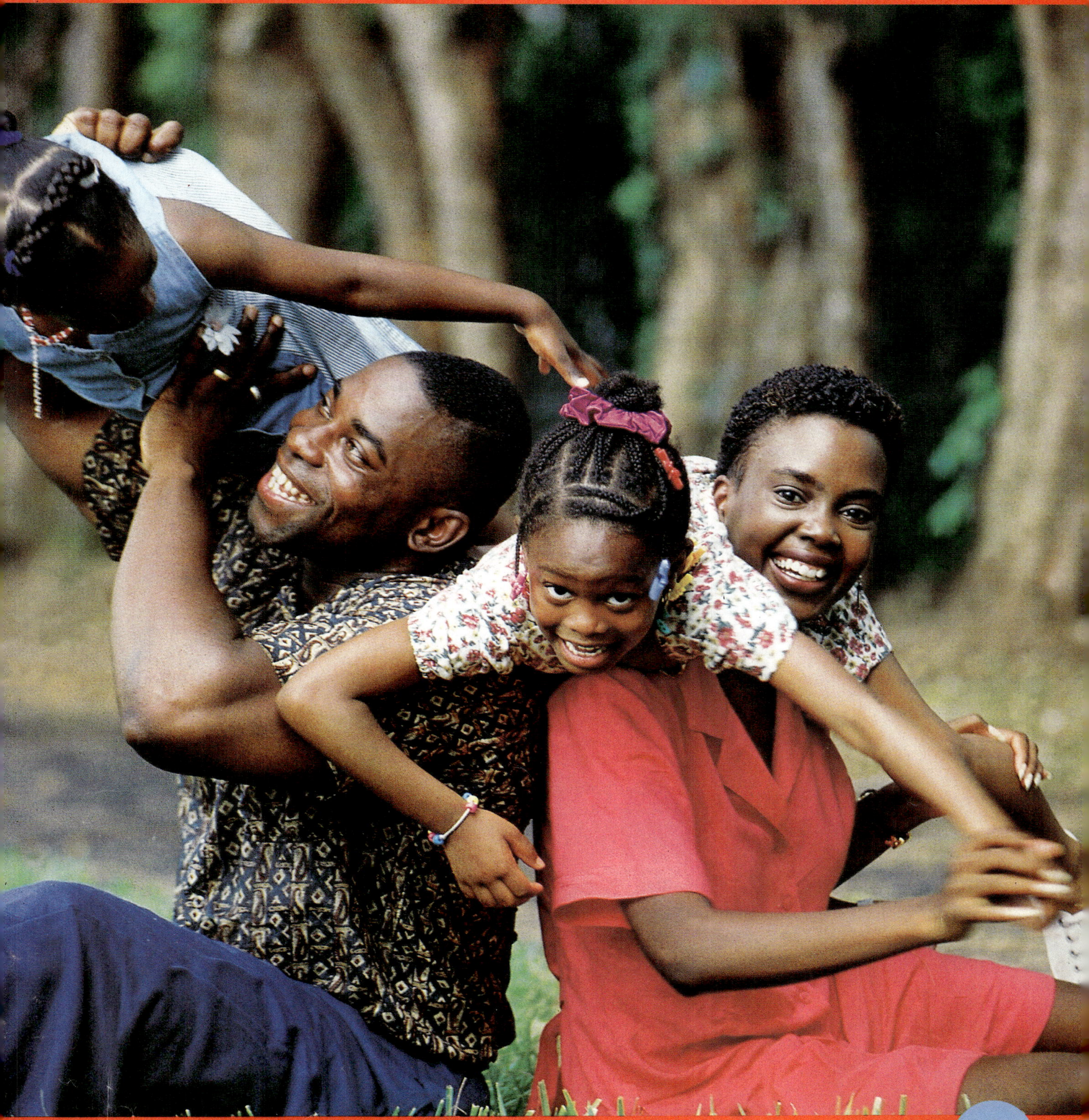

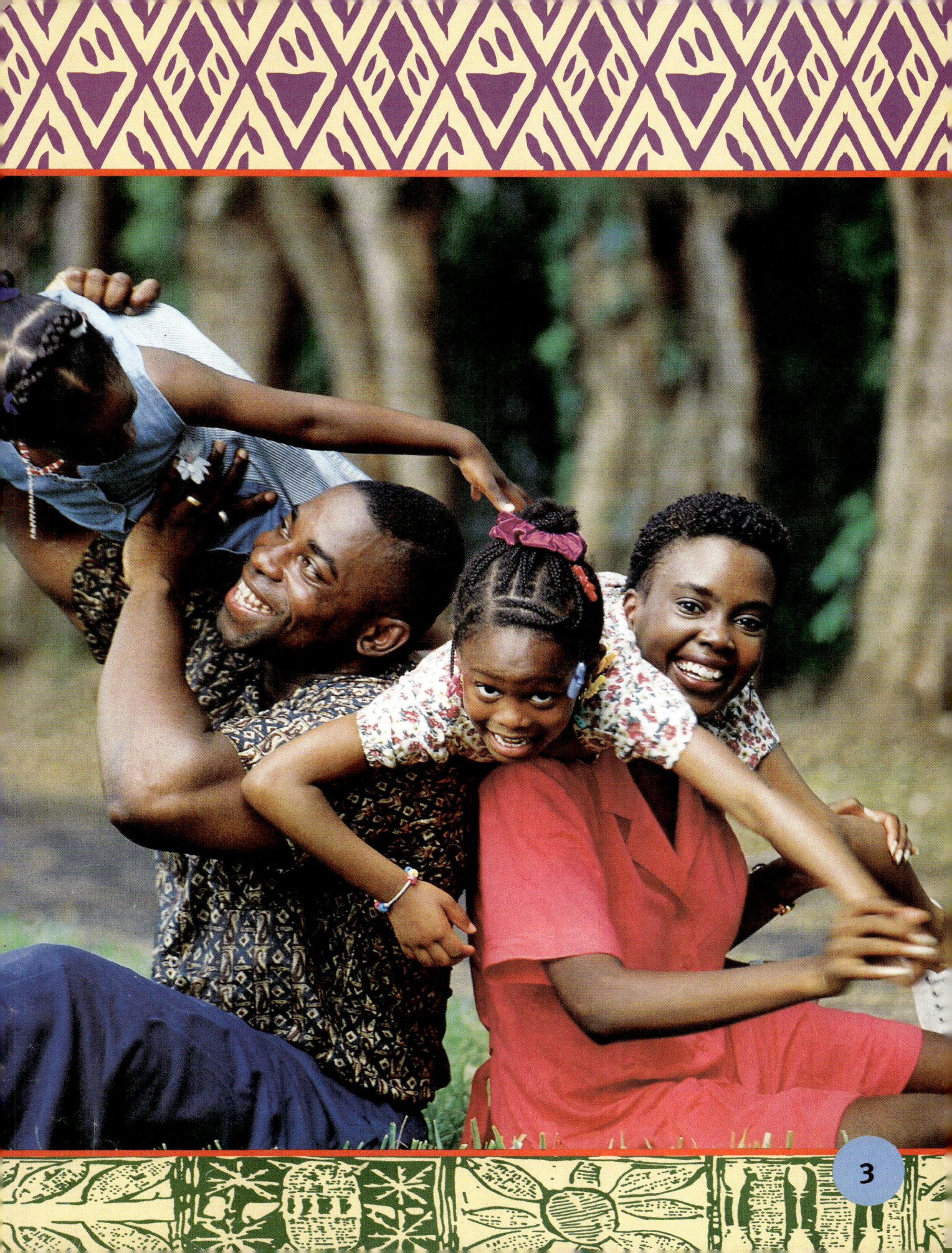

LESSON 1: WHAT KIND OF FAMILY DO YOU HAVE?

Sekou and Kimisha are brother and sister. Their family has four people. Their **family** is the people they live with. Sekou and Kimisha live with their mother and father.

Kevin lives with his grandfather. Grandfather takes good care of Kevin. They talk and eat and play together. Kevin likes his family just the way it is.

Rosa has a big family.
There are grandmothers
and grandfathers.
There are aunts and
uncles and cousins.

Angela has a big family, too. Grandpa had a birthday. Angela's whole family came to the party. Mom made a cake for Grandpa. Everybody had a good time.

What kind of family do you have?

LESSON 2: FAMILIES CARE

Families give love. They help us see the good things about ourselves. Maya tells her grandmother about her day at school. Grandmother listens to Maya. This is one way family members show that they care.

Tiffany wants to learn how to swim. Her aunt helps her do things that are new to her. Her family makes time for Tiffany. This is another way that families show that they care.

Who helps you in your family?

LESSON 3: RULES HELP FAMILIES

Families have rules to keep children healthy and safe. **Rules** tell us what to do and what not to do. Randy's mother teaches him rules for crossing the street. He looks both ways before he crosses. He looks to see if the light is green.

Lian knows the bedtime rules. She puts away her clothes and toys. She washes her face and brushes her teeth. She goes to bed at eight o'clock. She needs to get a good night's sleep.

1. What is one rule you follow when you are outside? How does it keep you safe?
2. What is one of your bedtime rules?

SKILLS Unit 1

Looking Down

This is a bedroom for two children.
It has two beds.
It has two bookcases.
Can you find the two dressers?

How would the room look from up high?

Point to the beds.

Point to the bookcases.

What else do you see?

LESSON 4: A FAMILY IS A TEAM

Darla loves to go shopping with her dad. They are at the market buying vegetables. They will buy flowers, too. It feels good to work together.

14

In Tai's family, everybody helps with dinner. Today they made soup. Now the family will enjoy eating together.

There are many chores to do. Everybody in Philip's family helps. Philip folds the clothes. He likes to help his family. They are a team.

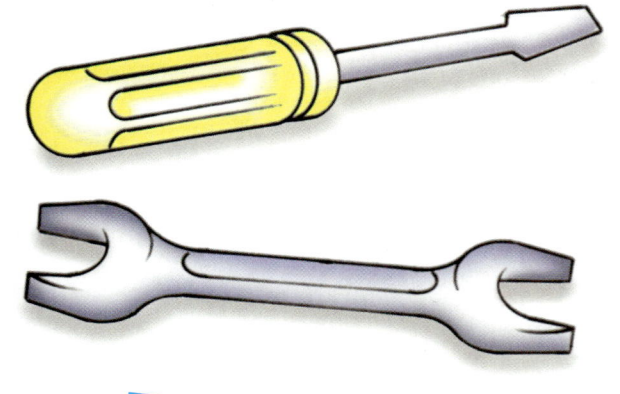

Justin's bike broke. His dad will help him fix it. Dad shows Justin how to use the tools. They work together on the bike.

1. How do you help in your family?
2. How does your family work as a team?

SKILLS Unit 1

Using Maps

This picture shows the rooms in Philip's home. It shows what they would look like from up high.

Point to the kitchen.

18

This is a map of Philip's home. A **map** is a drawing. It shows how a place would look from up high. We can use a map to find places. The children's bedroom is next to the living room.

Use the map to answer these questions.

1. How many bedrooms are in Philip's home?

2. Which rooms are next to the bathroom?

3. Is the children's bedroom near or far from the parents' bedroom?

LESSON 5: SOLVING FAMILY PROBLEMS

My brother and I had a problem. He wanted to eat the whole pizza. I wanted some pizza, too. I took the pizza away from him. I was angry with him. He was angry with me.

We decided to share the pizza. He has his own slice. I have my own slice. There is enough pizza for both of us. Sometimes when we solve a problem, we both get what we want.

How do you solve problems in your family?

REVIEW
Unit 1

Word Wrap

Use these words to complete the sentences.

    rule   family   map

1. My _____ helps me learn new things.

2. A _____ is a drawing of a place.

3. A _____ can tell us how to behave outside.

Unit Wrap

Family members are alike in many ways. Families learn from each other. They work together and solve problems. Families show their love.

1. What is one way that families are alike?

2. What is special about your family?

REVIEW SKILLS

Looking Down

This is a picture of a lobby. It is in our apartment house. Use it to answer the questions.

1. Point to the two sofas.
2. Point to the front door.
3. Can you find two plants?
4. What is next to the door?

23

Unit 2

WE ARE A FAMILY AT SCHOOL

Tyrell is on his way to school. At school he makes new friends. He meets his teachers. He learns new things.

25

LESSON 1

NEW FRIENDS

This is our school. We all learn together here. It is fun to find out new things.

We meet new friends in our classroom. This year we are learning to read. We are learning to write stories, too. We are learning about places near and far.

We have fun on the school playground. We play with all our new friends. They are part of our school family. People in a school family have fun together. They help each other, too.

We take turns playing on the swing. When the bell rings, we all go inside. Then we learn with all our new friends.

What do new friends do at school?

SKILLS
Unit 2

Using Map Keys

Maps use symbols. A symbol is a drawing that stands for something. Symbols can help people find things easily. What do you think these symbols stand for?

Maps that use symbols have a **map key**. The map key tells what each symbol stands for.

This map shows Darla's neighborhood. Use the map and the map key to answer the questions.

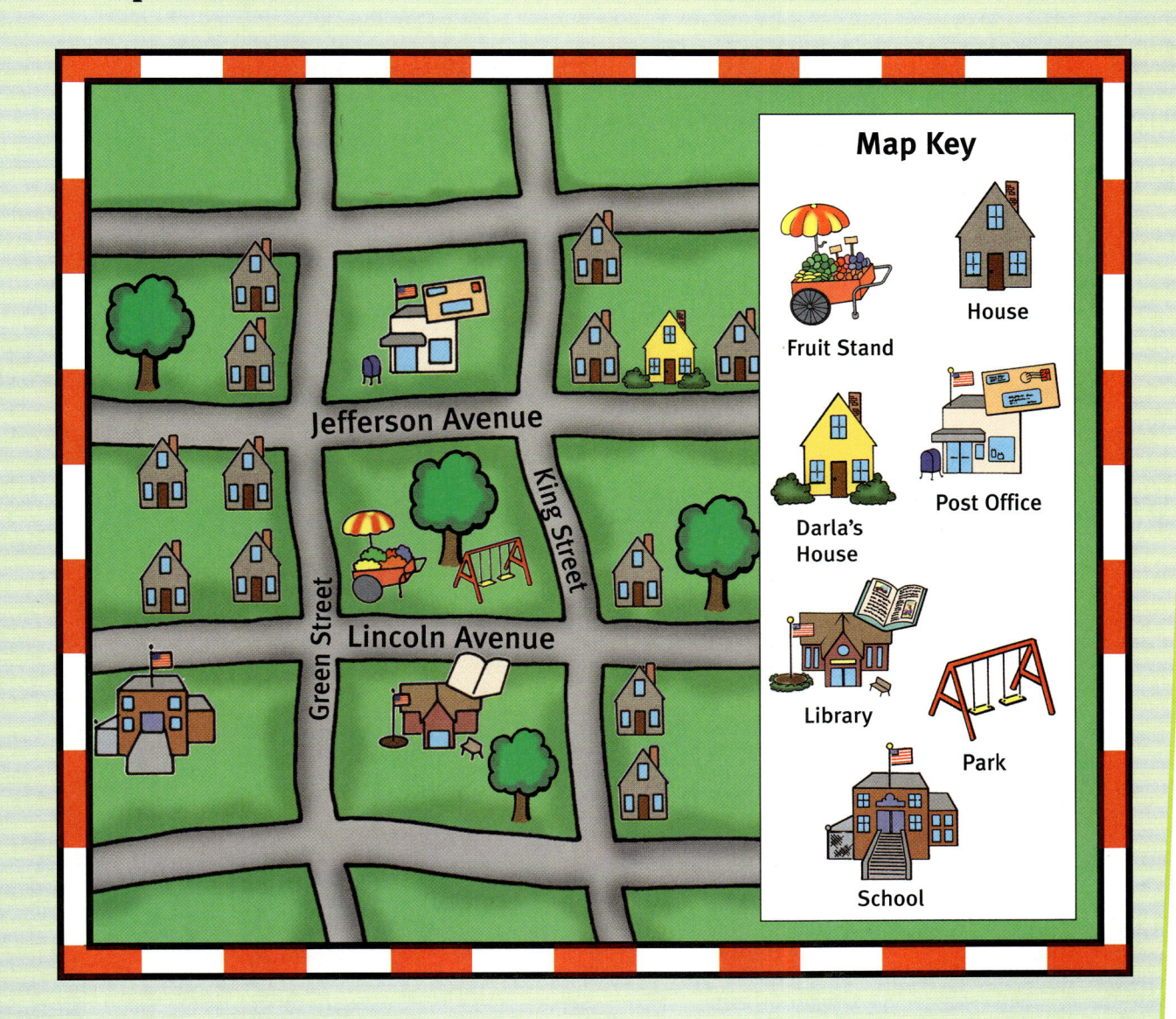

1. What symbols are used on this map?

2. Can you find the school on the map key and on the map?

3. What street is Darla's house on?

LESSON 2: OUR SCHOOL FAMILY CARES FOR US

Mrs. Jones is our teacher. To begin each day, she says, "Good morning, class!" We are happy to see her. She teaches us to write the alphabet. We ask her questions.

Many people help take care of us at school.
Mr. Brant teaches us about computers.
We see Mr. Brant in the media center.

We see the school principal in the hall.
She stops to talk with us. The principal
makes sure the school runs well.
She makes rules that keep us safe.

The janitor helps keep the school clean. There are other school workers, too. They work in the school office. They work in the lunchroom. All of them are part of our school family.

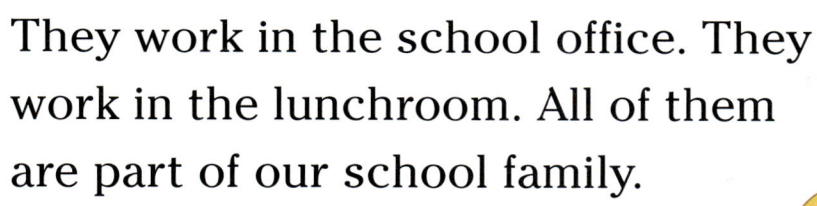

Who is part of your school family?

LESSON 3: HOME AND SCHOOL TOGETHER

Home families and school families work together in many ways. Devante's dad visits his school. He meets Devante's teacher. He asks the teacher how Devante is doing in class.

Sometimes adults help out in the classroom. Lisa's mother and Meisha's aunt help students learn to read.

These family members came to school to talk about their work. Mary's uncle shows the students how to juggle. He is a performer.

Lily's grandmother reads the class a story. She is a storyteller.

Latifa's godmother tells the class about Nigeria. She is a history teacher.

How does your home family work with your school family?

LESSON 4 RULES AT SCHOOL

Rules make the school a better place. I raise my hand when I want to talk. We do not all talk at once.

We follow the rules when we go on a field trip. We stay together. We hold hands with a partner. We listen to our teacher.

We follow rules in our classroom.
Books go back on the shelf.
There is a place for everything.
Blocks go back in the basket.

We have rules that help us work together.
Today we share our paint and brushes.
Sometimes we have to wait our turn.

What school rules do you follow?

SKILLS
Unit 2

Finding Directions on a Map

This is a map of the United States. The arrows on the map show north, south, east, and west.

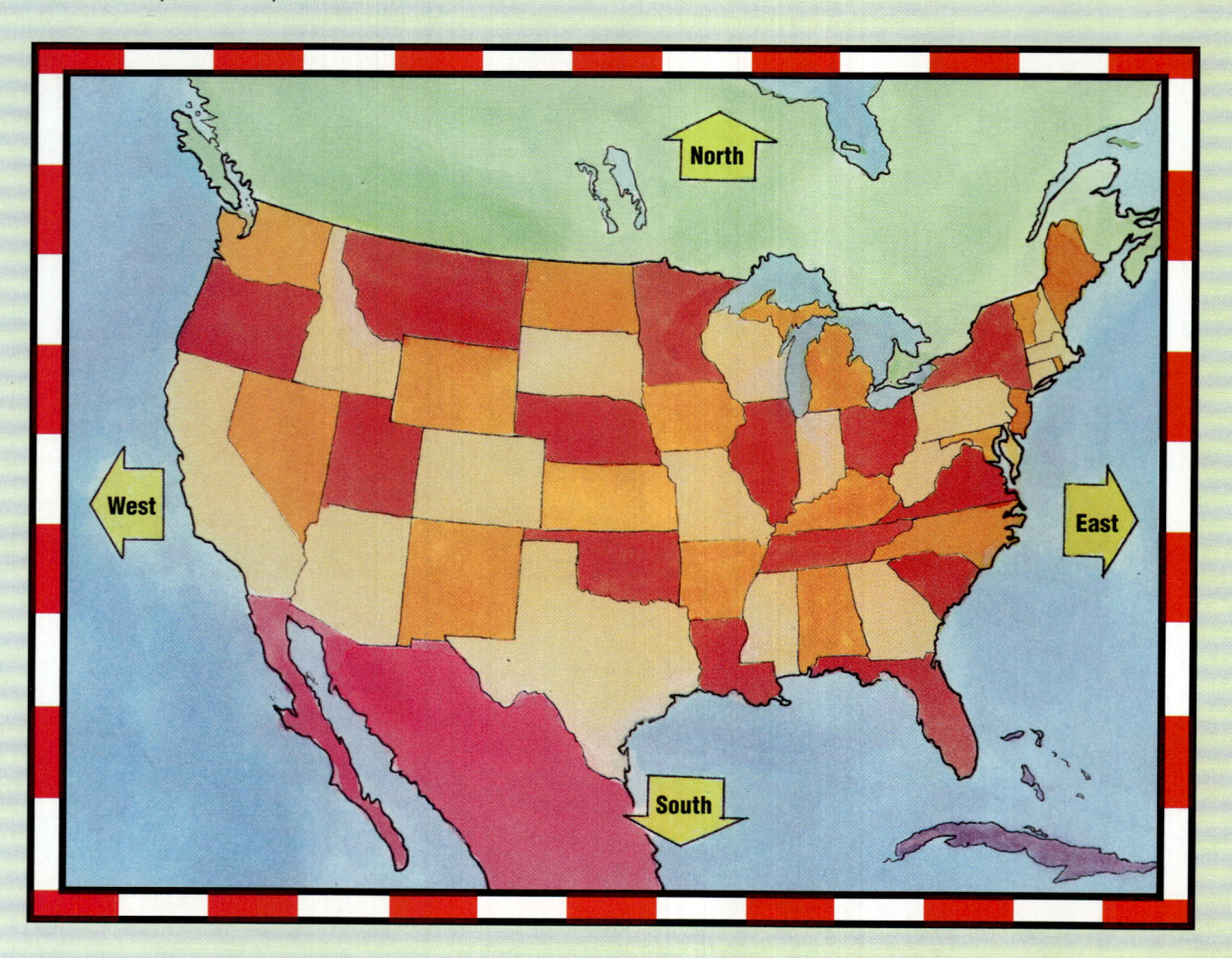

Find the arrow that points east.

44

Martin lives in Detroit. He has four pen pals. Today he is mailing four letters, one to each of his pen pals.

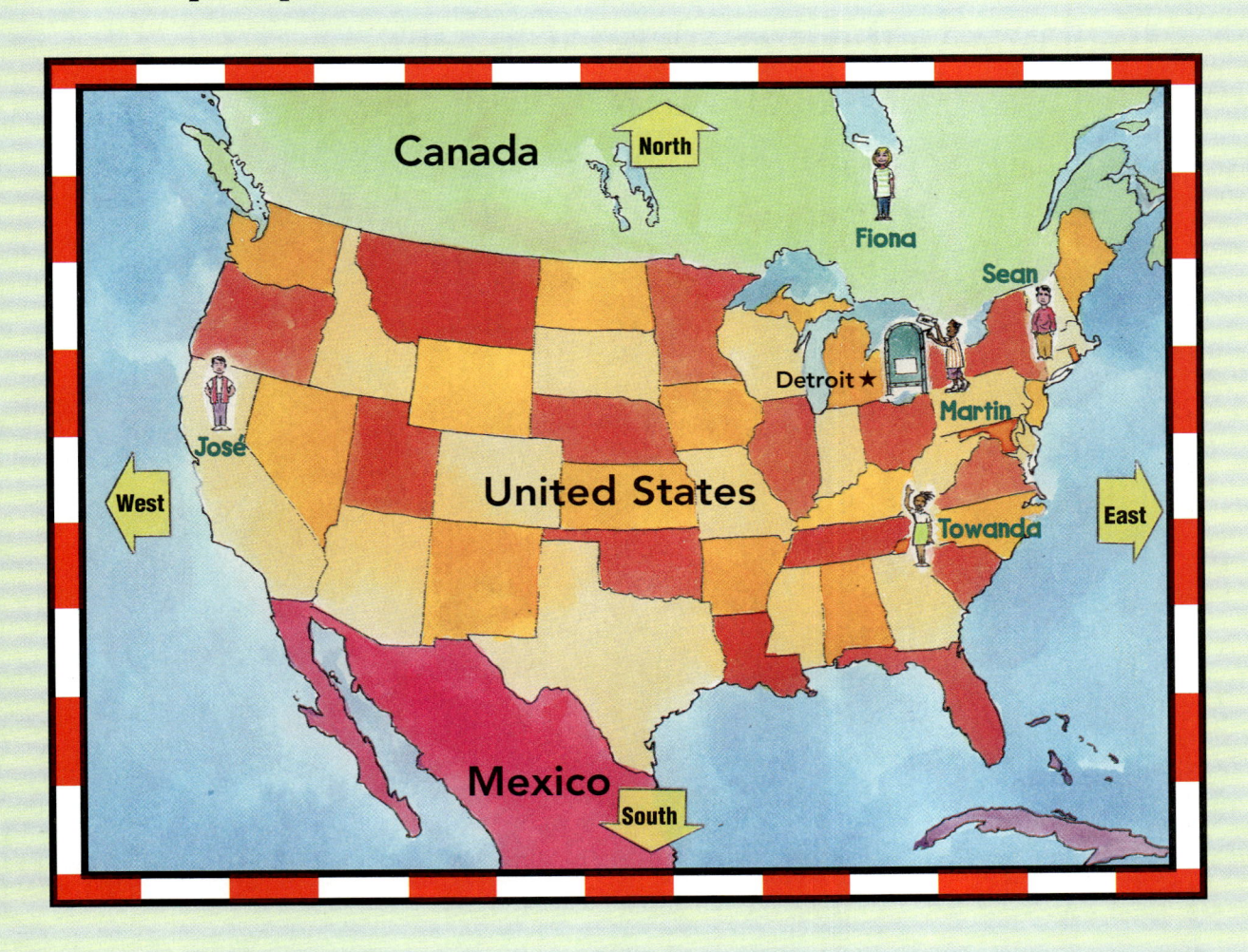

1 One letter is going south. Who will get it?

2 One is going to José. Which way will it go?

3 One is going east. Who will get it?

4 One is going to Canada. Which way will it go? Who will get it?

LESSON 5: SOLVING PROBLEMS AT SCHOOL

Carlos and Kevin have a problem. They both want to play with the fire truck. Carlos and Kevin are upset with each other. Carlos asks their teacher to help them decide what to do.

Carlos and Kevin decide to take turns playing with the fire truck. First, Carlos plays with the fire truck. Kevin plays with another toy. Kevin plays with the fire truck later.

How do you solve problems at school?

SKILLS Unit 2

Using Charts

Charts show information in a simple way. The title tells what the chart is about.

Books We Have Read

	Chris	Tyrell	Allen	Keisha
My New Friend		★	★	★
Fun at School	★			★
The Yellow School Bus	★	★	★	★

Which children read My New Friend?

We can look at the chart.

We see that Tyrell, Keisha, and Allen read My New Friend.

Which book did all the children read?

48

This chart shows how the children will help.
Use the chart to answer the questions.

How We Help in Class

	Feed Goldfish	Pass Out Paper and Crayons	Clean Chalkboard	Collect Homework
Sharonda				🙂
Kwame	🙂			
Darrin			🙂	
Maggie		🙂		

1. How many ways are there to help in the classroom?

2. How will Sharonda help?

3. How will Kwame help?

4. Who will help by cleaning the chalkboard?

5. Who will pass out paper and crayons?

49

REVIEW
Unit 2

Unit Wrap

At school, we make new friends. We meet new people that care for us. At school, we learn to read and write together. We learn school rules. We learn to solve problems, too. At school we are like one big family.

Word Wrap

Use these words to complete the sentences.

directions **map key**
symbols

❶ You use a _____ to read a map.

❷ A map key uses _____ to stand for real things.

❸ North, south, east, and west are four _____.

How does your school family care for you?

REVIEW SKILLS

Map Keys

This is a neighborhood playground. Maps help you see whether things are near or far from each other. Use the map and the map key to answer the questions.

1 Kwame is playing in the sandbox. Is the sandbox close to the seesaw or far from the seesaw?

2 Kevin is on the swings. He wants to go on the slide and on the seesaw. Which is closer?

Unit 3

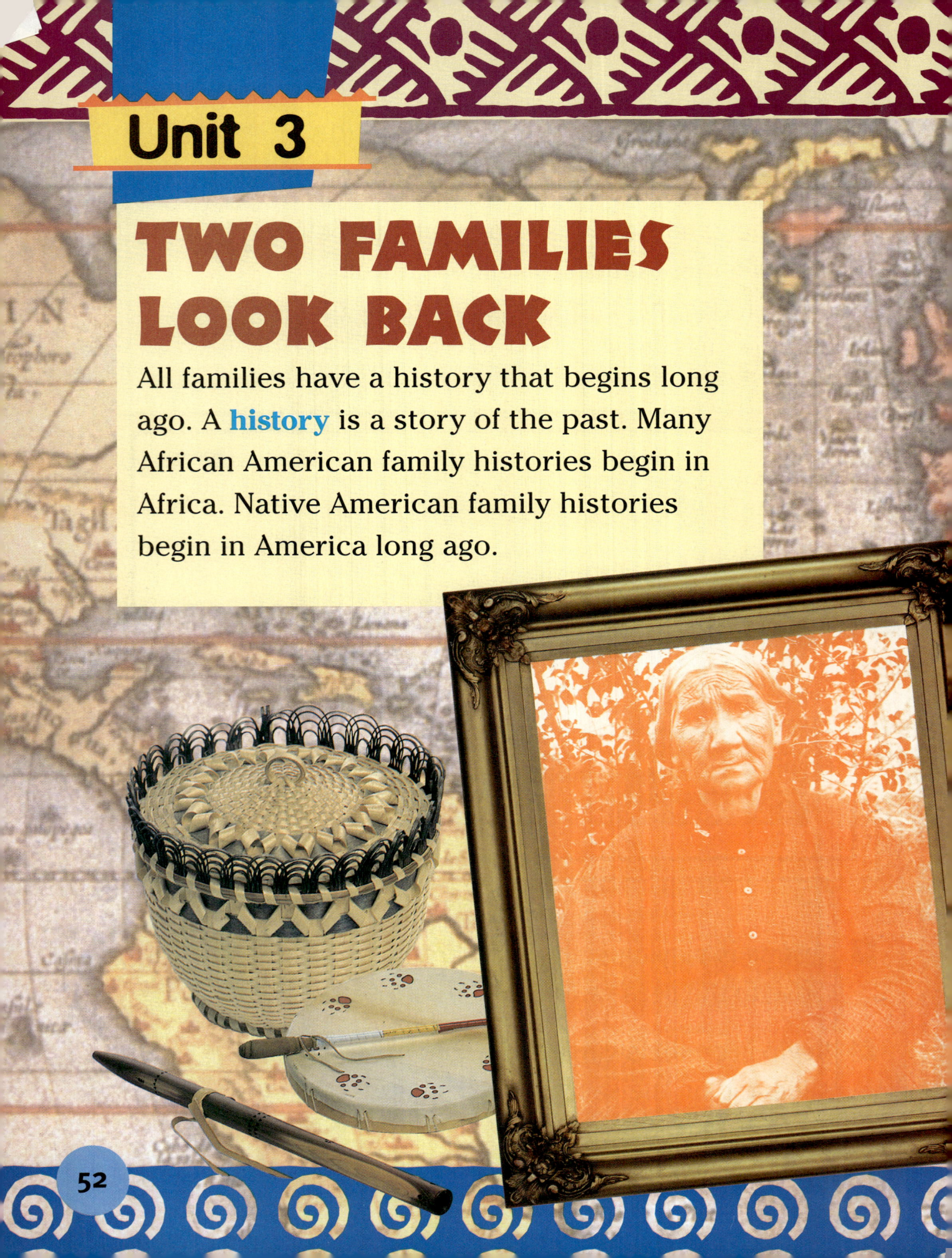

TWO FAMILIES LOOK BACK

All families have a history that begins long ago. A **history** is a story of the past. Many African American family histories begin in Africa. Native American family histories begin in America long ago.

53

LESSON 1
OUR STORY: A CHIPPEWA FAMILY

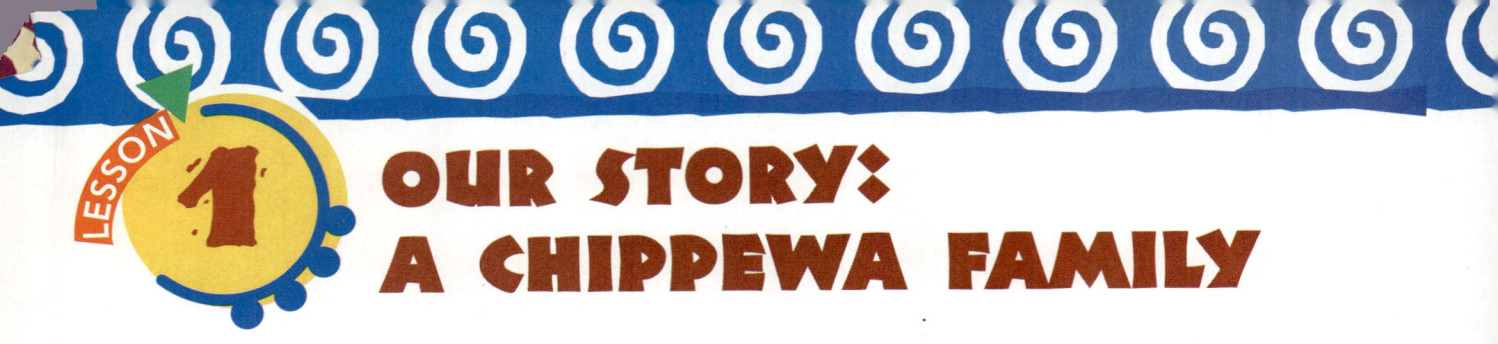

Native Americans were the first people to live here. My family is Chippewa. Each year my family goes to a powwow. A powwow is a big celebration.

This year at the powwow, Grandmother taught me to play a Chippewa flute. I did a dance that my grandmother's grandmother knew. Women brought baskets and clothing they made.

At the powwow, we learned about Chippewa history. Long ago, the Chippewa had summer homes and winter homes. In summer, our ancestors built homes of wood and bark. They grew rice, beans, and squash. They hunted and fished.

In winter, our ancestors lived in warm tepees. In all seasons, they used natural resources to live. Water, plants, and other things from nature are **natural resources**. They used plants for food and medicine. They used animal skins for clothing. Learning about my history makes me feel strong.

What was life like long ago for the Chippewa?

LESSON 2 — MY FAMILY IN AFRICA

Grandmother told me our family history. Our family came from the continent of Africa. In Africa there were great pyramids. There were large mosques.

58

Our family lived in a small village. They raised animals and sold them to nearby villages.

One day strangers came to our family's village. They had guns. They stole everything our family owned. They set fire to the crops and homes. Many people were captured and enslaved.

They were forced into dark ships. They sailed for many, many days. No one knew where they were going. Many people died on the way.

1. Do you know your family history? What can you tell about it?

2. What can you tell about your grandmothers and grandfathers?

SKILLS
Unit 3

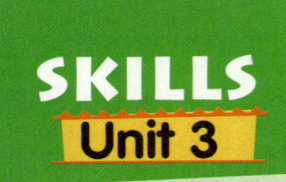

Finding the Main Idea

The **main idea** tells what a piece of writing is about. First read "The Continent of Africa."

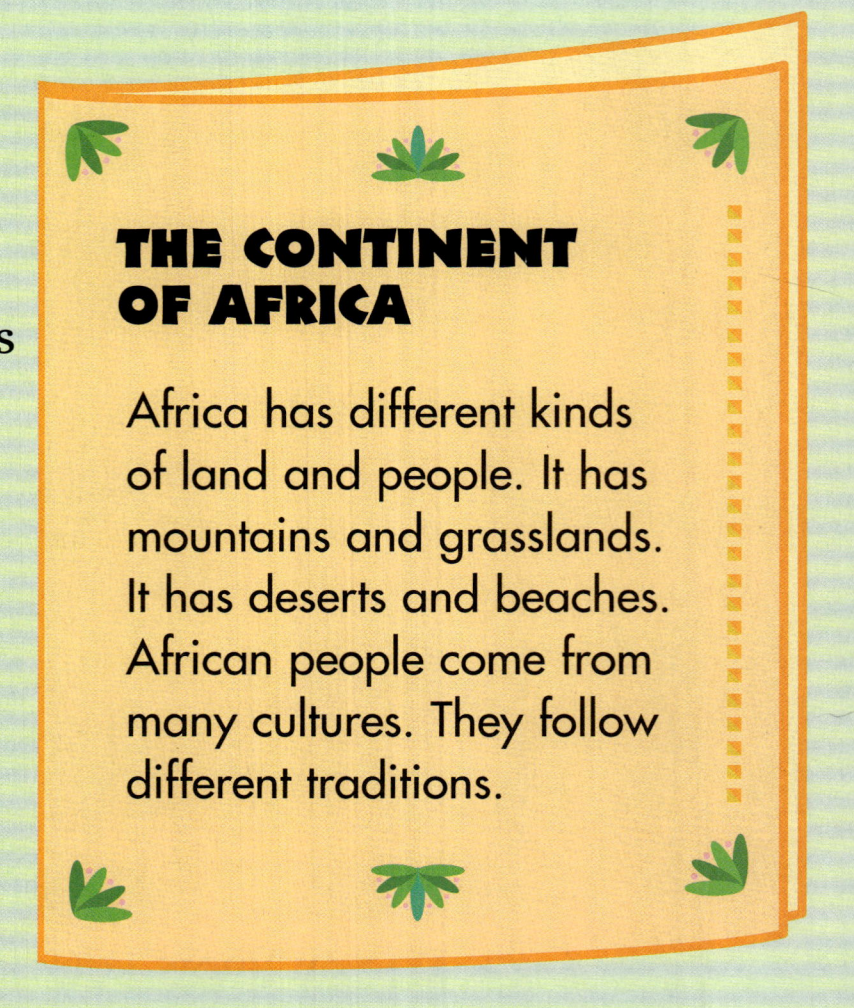

THE CONTINENT OF AFRICA

Africa has different kinds of land and people. It has mountains and grasslands. It has deserts and beaches. African people come from many cultures. They follow different traditions.

Sometimes the first sentence tells the main idea. This paragraph is about the land and people of Africa.

Now read the paragraph below.
Find the main idea.

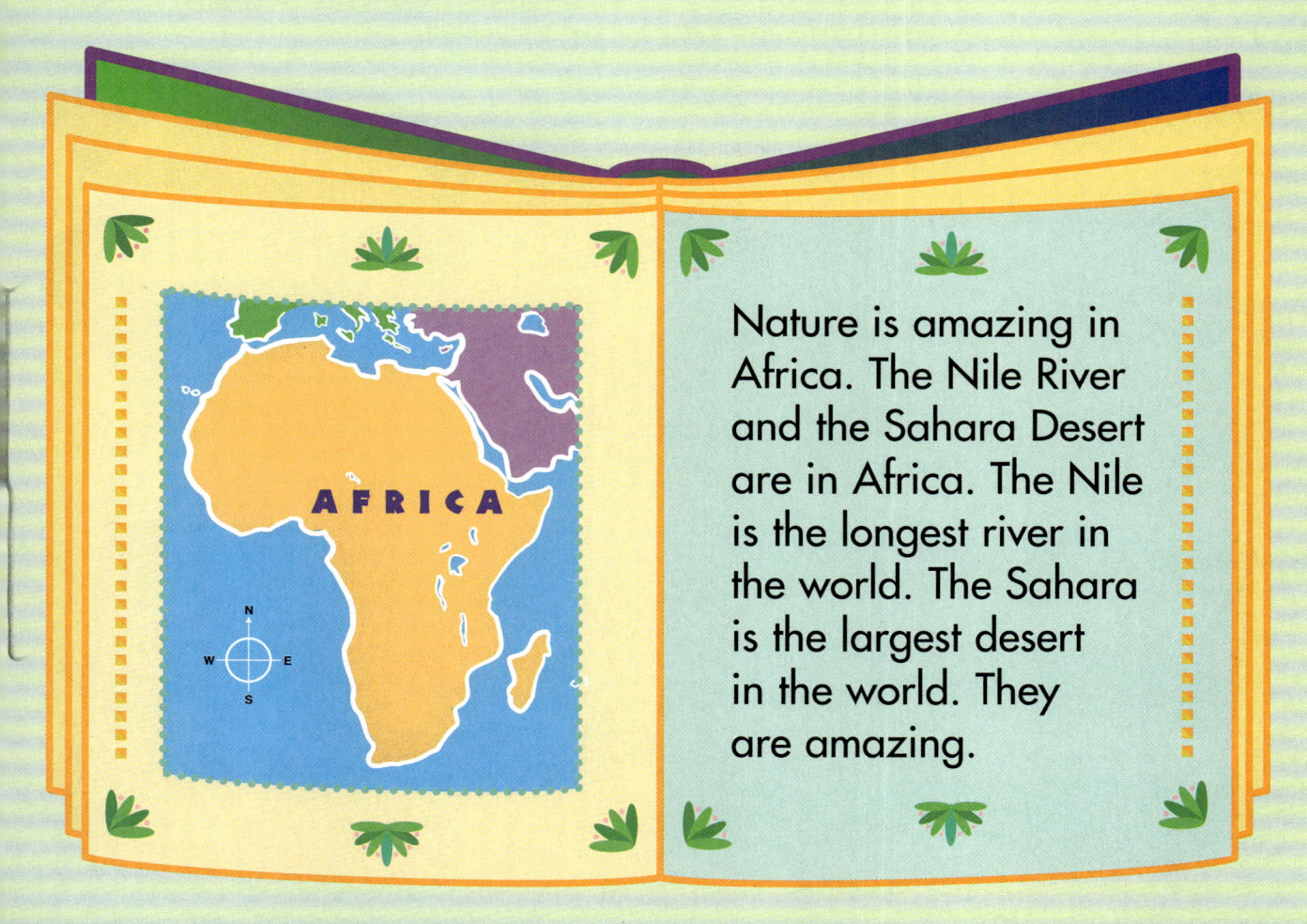

Nature is amazing in Africa. The Nile River and the Sahara Desert are in Africa. The Nile is the longest river in the world. The Sahara is the largest desert in the world. They are amazing.

1. What is the main idea?
2. What else did you learn about Africa?

LESSON 3
MY FAMILY IN EARLY AMERICA

Grandmother told me that some of the ships carrying our ancestors came to America. Our relatives were enslaved. To be enslaved means to work without pay.

My great-great-grandmother and grandfather were enslaved on a cotton farm. They ran away and took their own freedom. They told their story to all of our relatives.

What was life like for Africans in early America?

LESSON 4: MY FAMILY IN DETROIT

My grandmother's father grew up on a farm in the South. When he was a young man, he moved to Detroit to find better work. He wanted to make a good life for his children.

Grandmother's father found a place to live in a Detroit community. A **community** is a big neighborhood where people live and work together. He worked in a factory painting cars.

Grandmother's father and mother met at a church picnic. They were married in 1929. They raised four children. One of those children is my grandmother.

This year we celebrated my great-aunt and great-uncle's 50th wedding anniversary. At the celebration, we all joined hands. We said *Umoja*, which means "unity." Being united as a family makes me feel strong.

1. **Where do your grandparents, aunts, uncles, and cousins live?**
2. **How does your family celebrate important days?**

SKILLS Unit 3

Using Time Lines

A time line shows when things happened. This time line shows what Grandfather did over the years. Each mark on the time line stands for one year.

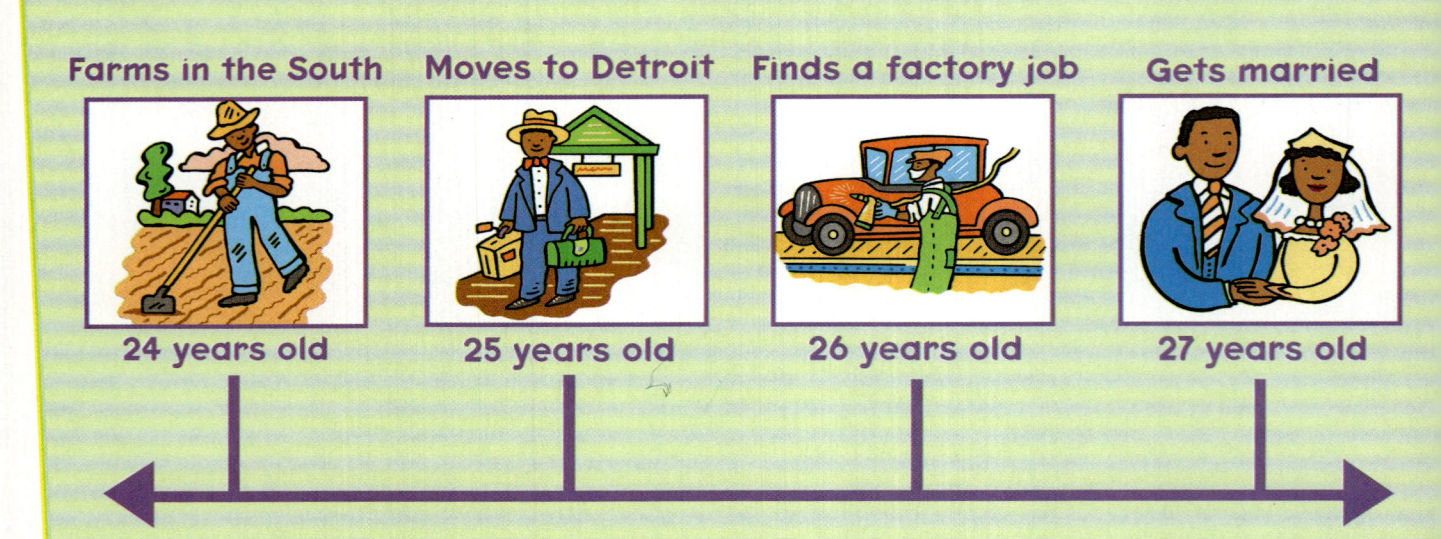

Farms in the South	Moves to Detroit	Finds a factory job	Gets married
24 years old	25 years old	26 years old	27 years old

When he was 25 years old, Grandfather moved to Detroit. What did Grandfather do when he was 26? How old was Grandfather when he got married?

This time line shows some things Edmund did over the years. Each mark on the time line stands for one year.

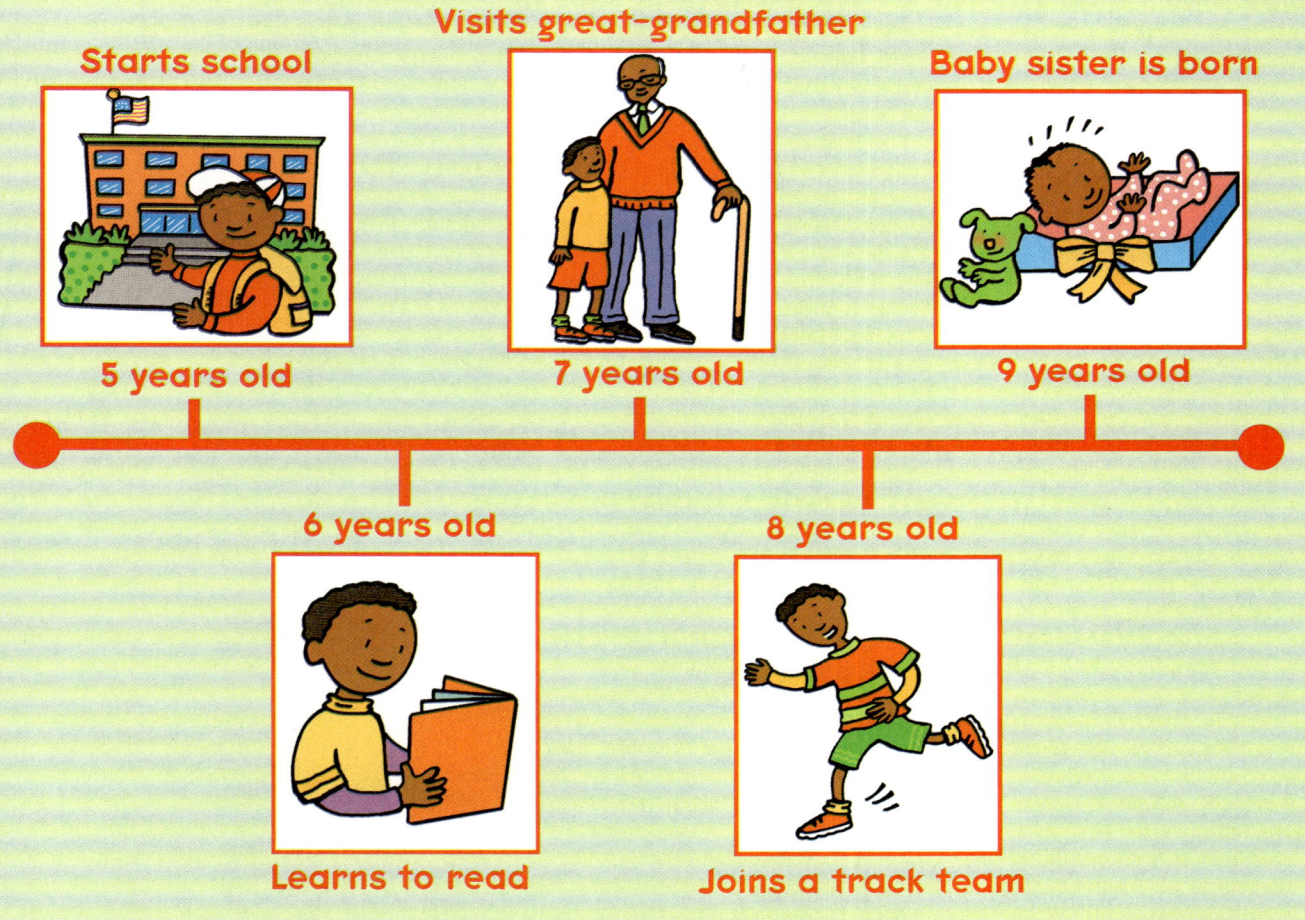

Starts school
5 years old

Visits great-grandfather
7 years old

Baby sister is born
9 years old

Learns to read
6 years old

Joins a track team
8 years old

Answer these questions. Use the time line.

1. How old was Edmund when he started school?

2. What did Edmund do when he was 7 years old?

3. How old was Edmund when his baby sister was born?

4. How would a time line help you remember things that happened?

71

SKILLS
Unit 3

Reading Photographs

Photographs can help us learn about the past. Look at the photograph. It tells us a lot.

There are people, cars, and buildings. Look at the clothes the people are wearing. How are the clothes different from clothes you see today? Look at the cars. How are they different? Was the photograph taken a long time ago?

The picture below is part of the big picture.

1 Look at the clothing the child is wearing. What can you tell about the weather? Was it very hot, very cold, or just cool?

2 What do you think the people in the picture are going to do next? What clues do you have?

3 Put yourself in this photograph. What would you be doing? What would you be wearing?

73

REVIEW
Unit 3

Word Wrap

Use these words to complete the sentences.

history **community** **main idea**

time line **natural resource**

1. Water is one _____.

2. The people in my _____ live and work together.

3. My family _____ tells the story of my family's past.

4. A _____ shows when things happened.

5. The _____ is the most important idea.

Unit Wrap

A family history tells about traditions. It tells about where a family began. It tells about how a family moved, worked, and married. It tells how a family made a better life for their children and grandchildren.

1. Can you name one place that your ancestors came from?

2. Can you tell a story from your family's history?

REVIEW SKILLS

Using Time Lines

A time line shows when things happened. This time line shows the early years of Camella's life. Each mark on the time line stands for one year. Use the time line to answer the questions.

Grandmother visits
2 years old

Moves to a new house
4 years old

Gets first pet
3 years old

Learns to tie her shoes
5 years old

1. How old was Camella when she learned to tie her shoes?

2. What happened when Camella was three?

3. How old was Camella when she moved into a new house?

75

The United States

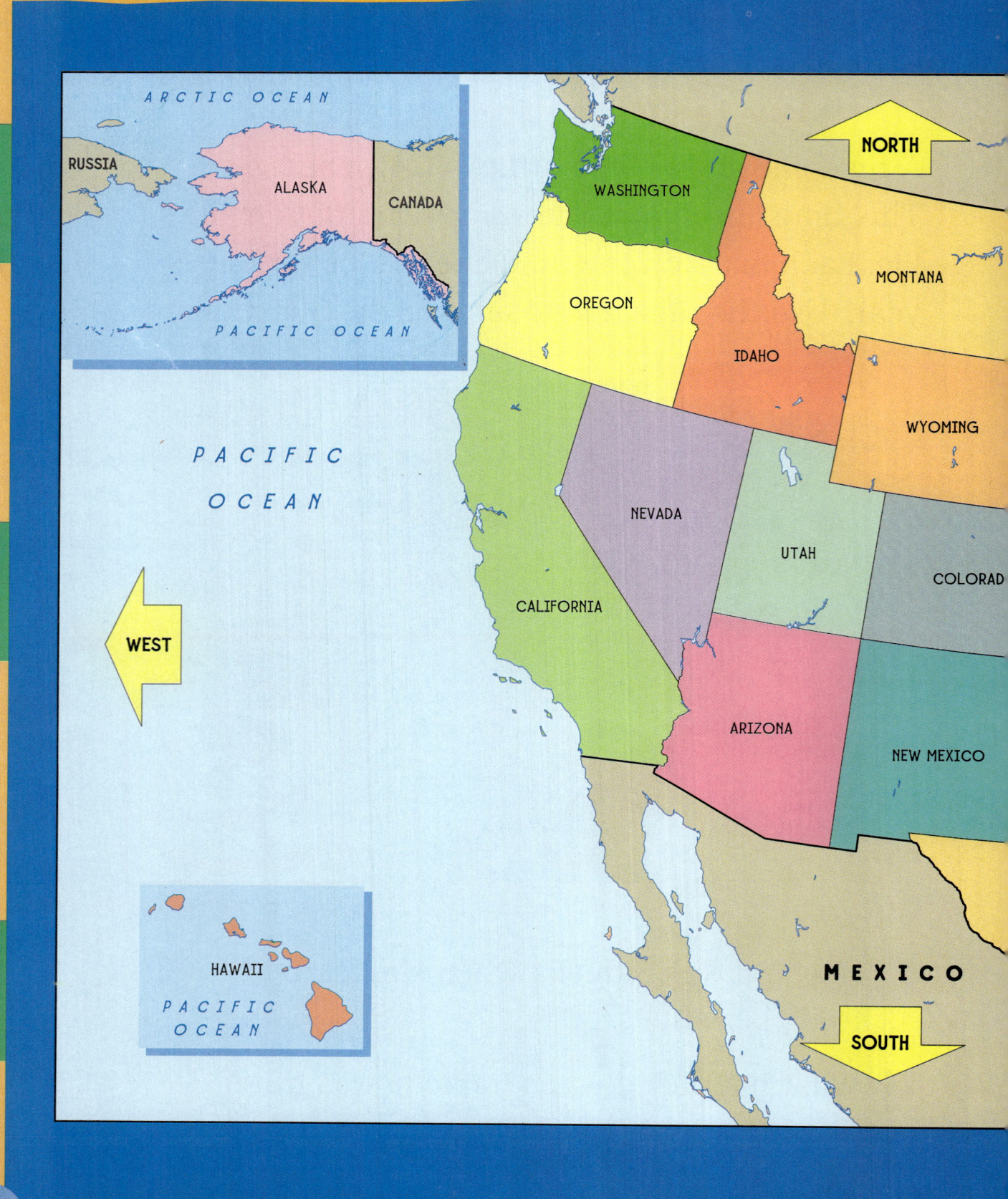

ARCTIC OCEAN

RUSSIA
ALASKA
CANADA
PACIFIC OCEAN

PACIFIC OCEAN

WEST

HAWAII
PACIFIC OCEAN

NORTH

WASHINGTON
OREGON
IDAHO
MONTANA
WYOMING
NEVADA
UTAH
CALIFORNIA
COLORADO
ARIZONA
NEW MEXICO

MEXICO

SOUTH

ATLAS

CANADA

- H DAKOTA
- MINNESOTA
- H DAKOTA
- WISCONSIN
- Lake Superior
- Lake Huron
- Lake Michigan
- MICHIGAN
- Lake Ontario
- MAINE
- VERMONT
- NEW HAMPSHIRE
- NEW YORK
- MASSACHUSETTS
- RHODE ISLAND
- CONNECTICUT
- NEBRASKA
- IOWA
- Lake Erie
- PENNSYLVANIA
- NEW JERSEY
- ILLINOIS
- INDIANA
- OHIO
- Washington, D. C. ★
- DELAWARE
- WEST VIRGINIA
- MARYLAND
- KANSAS
- MISSOURI
- KENTUCKY
- VIRGINIA
- NORTH CAROLINA
- OKLAHOMA
- ARKANSAS
- TENNESSEE
- SOUTH CAROLINA
- MISSISSIPPI
- ALABAMA
- GEORGIA
- TEXAS
- LOUISIANA
- FLORIDA

ATLANTIC OCEAN

→ EAST

★ National capital

R3

The World

ARCTIC OCEAN

NORTH AMERICA

UNITED STATES

NORTH

PACIFIC OCEAN

ATLANTIC OCEAN

WEST

SOUTH AMERICA

SOUTH

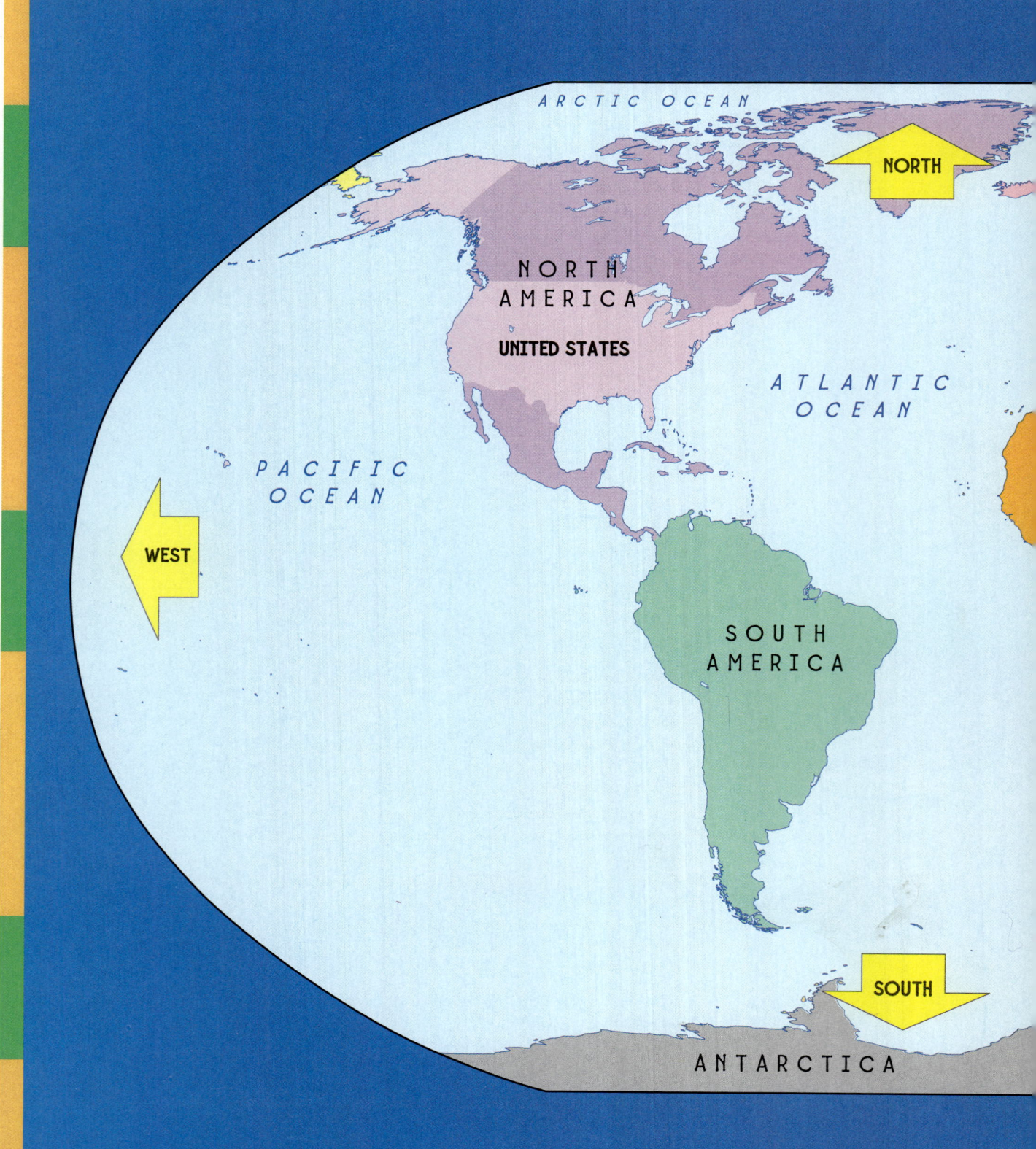

ANTARCTICA

ATLAS

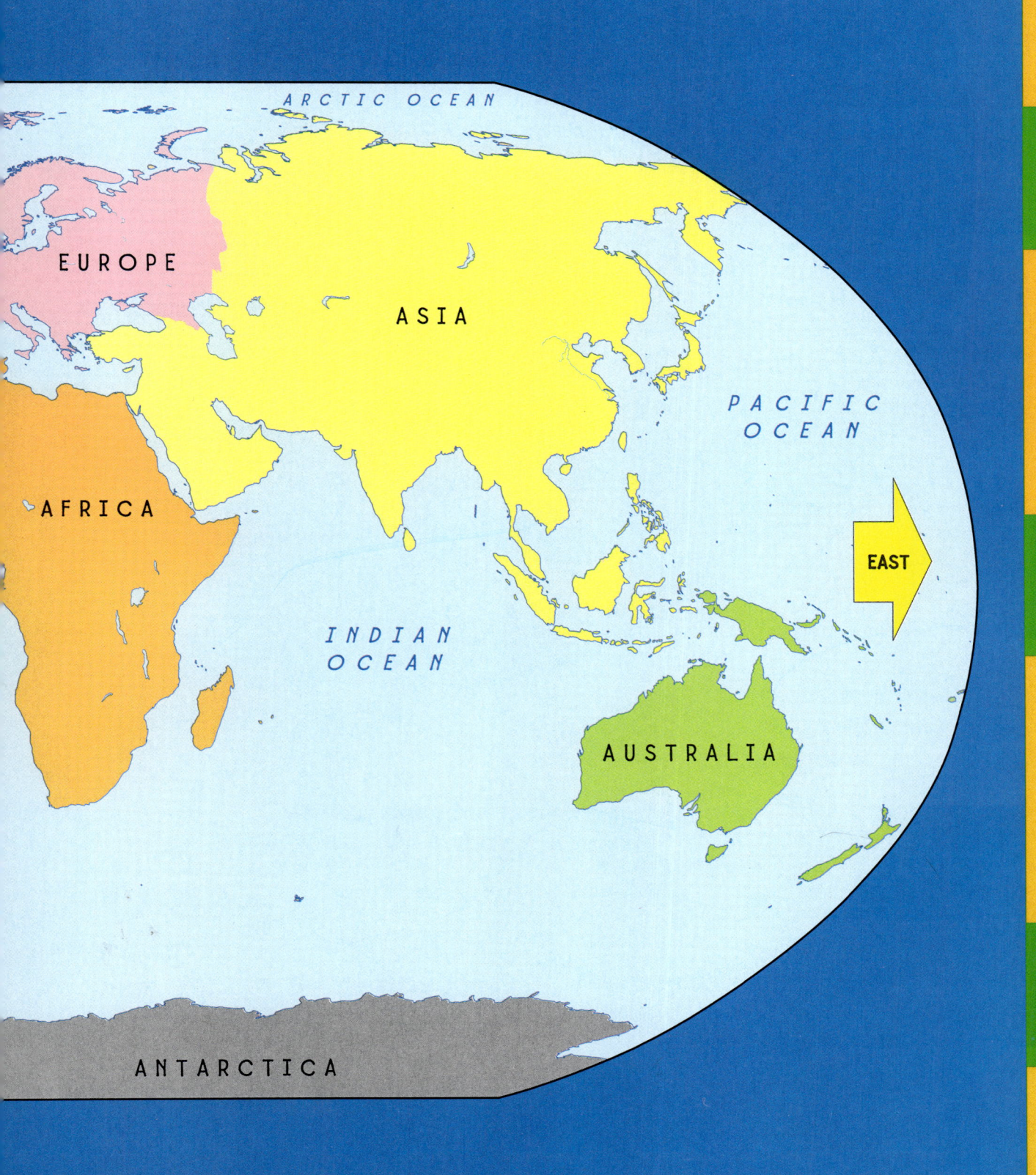

ARCTIC OCEAN

EUROPE

ASIA

AFRICA

PACIFIC OCEAN

EAST

INDIAN OCEAN

AUSTRALIA

ANTARCTICA

R5

Dictionary of Geographic Words

mountain – the tallest kind of land

valley – low land between hills or mountains

river – a long body of water that flows downhill

hill – raised land smaller than a mountain

ocean – the biggest kind of body of water

plain – flat land

lake – water that has land all around it

R7

GRADE 1

BAR GRAPH a chart that uses bars to show "how many." *The* bar graph *shows how many books we read.*

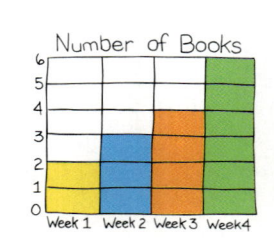

CALENDAR a chart that shows the months, weeks, and days of the year. *I use a* calendar *to find out what day it is.*

CHART a way to show facts using words and a picture. *The* chart *shows that more people like jelly.*

CITIZEN a person who lives in a country. *He is a* citizen *of the United States.*

COMMUNITY people who have the same interests; people who live in the same area. *Many people live in my* community.

CONTINENT the largest kind of land area. *North America is a* continent.

R8

COUNTRY a land shared by a group of people. *The United States is our* country.

DIRECTION North, south, east, and west are directions. *The direction of Mexico is south of the United States.*

EARTH the planet we live on. *The United States is on planet* Earth.

FAMILY the people you live with. *My* family *lives in a big house.*

GOODS things that people make or grow to sell. *The store sells* goods *like fruits and pots.*

HISTORY a true story about things that happened long ago. History *is a story about the past.*

LAW a rule that leaders make for people. *A* law *helped to end slavery.*

MAIN IDEA the most important idea of a story. *The main idea is the most important idea.*

MAP a drawing of a place. *The map shows a country.*

MAP KEY a chart that helps people read a map. *The map shows a red box. The map key shows it is a school.*

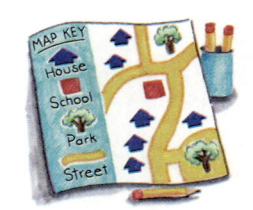

MONTH a part of a year. *We have a holiday in the month of January.*

NATURAL RESOURCES things people use that come from nature. *Water and soil are natural resources.*

NEEDS things that people must have to live. *Food, a home, and clothing are needs.*

NEIGHBORHOOD an area within a town or city where people work, live, and play. *My neighborhood has two parks.*

PICTURE GRAPH a way to show "how many" using pictures. *The* picture graph *shows how many animals.*

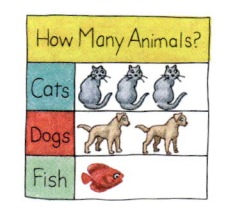

PLAIN a kind of land that is flat. *The* plain *ended at the mountains.*

PREDICTION a good guess about something that might happen. *My* prediction *is that it will rain.*

PRESIDENT the leader of the United States. *George Washington was our first* President.

RECYCLE to collect something and reuse it. *We* recycle *paper, plastic, glass, and metal.*

RULE something that tells people how to behave. *The* rule *in the library is to be quiet.*

SEASON a time of year. *There are four* seasons *in the year.*

SERVICE something that people do to help others. *The firefighters give us* service *by putting out fires.*

SHELTER a place where people or animals live. *An apartment building is one kind of* shelter.

SLAVERY when people are owned by others. *In the time of* slavery, *people were owned and sold.*

STATE a large area that is part of a country. *Michigan is a* state *in our country.*

SYMBOL something that stands for something else. *The American flag is a* symbol *of the United States.*

TIME LINE a chart that shows when things happened. *My* time line *shows how I grew.*

TRANSPORTATION a way of moving people and things. *A bus is a kind of* transportation.

R12

VOLUNTEER a person who decides to be a helper. *The* volunteer *passes out lunch.*

VOTE a fair way to decide or choose something. *We had a* vote *for class helper.*

WANTS things people like, but do not need to live. *I do not need a bicycle, but it is one of my* wants.

WEATHER the kind of air outside. *The* weather *today is hot.*

GRADE 1

INDEX

A

Africa, 52, 58–63
    cities of, 59
    continent of, 62–63
    nature and, 63
    villages, 58, 60
African Americans
    family of, 52–69
    slavery and, 60–61, 64–65
Ancestors
    African American, 52, 58–69
    Native American, 52, 56–57
Aunts, 6

B

Bedtime, 11

C

Careers, 35, 38–39
Caring, 8–9, 32–35
Charts, using, 48–49
Chippewa, 54–57
Chores, 14–17
City, 59, 66, 70–71
Classroom, 27, 36–37
Community, 67
Computers, 33
Cousins, 6

D

Detroit, Michigan, 66, 70–71
Directions, finding on a map, 44–45

F

Family, defined, 4
    histories of, 52
    kinds of, 4–7, 54, 56, 58
    problem solving and, 20–21
    rules and, 10–11
    school and, 24–50
    teamwork and, 14–17
Father, 4
Freedom, 64–65
Friendship, 24–29

G

Godmother, 39
Grandfather, 5–7, 65–68
Grandmother, 5–6, 8, 55, 58, 65–68

H

History, 52, 56, 58
Home families, 2–23, 36–37. See also Family.

L

Learning, 24, 27, 32, 33, 37

Looking down, 12, 13, 23
Love, 8–9

M

Main idea, finding, 62–63
Map, defined, 18–19
    finding directions on, 44–45
    United States, 44–45, R2–R3
Map key, using, 30–31, 51, 75
Michigan. See Detroit.
Mother, 4

N

Native American.
    See Chippewa.
Natural resources, 57
Neighborhood, 31, 67
Nile River, 63

P

Parents, 4, 17, 36–37
Pictures, reading, 72–73
Playground, 28–29
Powwow, 54–56
Principal, 34
Problem solving
    at home, 20–21
    at school, 46–47

R

Relatives.
    See Family and kinds of.
Rules, 10–11, 34, 40–43

S

Safety, 10, 34
Sahara Desert, 63
School, 24–50.
    See also Family.
Siblings, 4, 20–21
Slave ships, 61, 64
Slavery, 60–61, 64–65
Symbols, 30–31

T

Teachers, 24, 32–33, 36–37, 39, 46
Teamwork, 14–17, 43
Teepees, 57
Time lines, using, 72–73

U

Uncles, 6, 38
United States, map of, 44–45, R2–R3
Unity, 69

V

Village, 59

W

Work, 35, 38–39, 66. See also Careers; Chores.

R15

CREDITS

Art Credits
4, 6: Rich Colichio; 5: Virginia Graziano; 12, 13, 44, 45: Dennis Dittrich; 18, 19, 23, 30, 31, 51: Robert Steimle; 43, 62, 63: Michael Hortens; 56, 57: Rodica Prato; 58: Pamela Johnson; 60: Gershom Griffith; 70, 71, 75: Teresa Anderko; R6, R7: Neverne Covington; R8–R13: Mindy Mitchell

Photo Credits
Front Cover: (left, right, and bottom background) Stephen Ogilvy, (top center) George Shelley/The Stock Market, (center) T & D McCarthy/The Stock Market, (bottom center and top background) Gordon Alexander.

Back Cover: Gordon Alexander

Title Page: Stephen Ogilvy; iii: (bottom left) Bill Bachman/Photo Researchers, Inc., (top) George Shelley/The Stock Market, (bottom right) Gordon Alexander; iv: (top left) Leonard Crosby/The Detroit Public School System, (top right) John Weizenbach/The Stock Market, (bottom left) Leonard Crosby/The Detroit Public School System, (bottom right) John Chaisson/Gamma Liaison; v: (top left) Courtesy, Library of Congress, (top right) Corbis/Charles & Josette Lenars, (bottom left) From the Collections of Henry Ford Museum and Greenfield Village, (bottom right) Gordon Alexander; 2: (top) Gordon Alexander, (bottom) Susan Kuklin/Photo Researchers, Inc; 2–3: George Shelley/The Stock Market; 4: Bill Bachman/Photo Researchers, Inc.; 5: Farrell: Grehan/Photo Researchers, Inc.; 6: Chuck Savage/The Stock Market; 7: Michael Schwartz/The Image Works; 8: Peter Beck/The Stock Market; 9: George Shelley/The Stock Market; 10: Gary Landsman/The Stock Market; 11: John Fortunato; 14: (top right) Susan Kuklin/Photo Researchers, Inc., (top left and bottom) Gordon Alexander; 15: T & D McCarthy/The Stock Market; 16: Blair Seitz/Photo Reserchers, Inc.; 17: Jose L. Pelaez/The Stock Market; 20–21: Stephen Ogilvy; 22: Lawrence Migdale/Photo Researchers, Inc.; 24: Leonard Crosby/The Detroit Public School System; 24–25: John Weizenbach/The Stock Market; 25, 26: John Chaisson/Gamma Liaison; 26–27: Leonard Crosby/The Detroit Public School System; 28–29: Bob Daemmrich/Stock Boston; 29: Bob Daemmrich/The Image Works; 32: Peter Beck/The Stock Market; 33: (all photographs) Leonard Crosby/The Detroit Public School System; 34: Kate Denny/PhotoEdit; 35: Tony Freeman/PhotoEdit; 36: Robin L. Sachs/PhotoEdit; 37: David M. Grossman/Photo Researchers, Inc.; 38: Esther Shatavsky; 38–39: Leonard Crosby/The Detroit Public School System; 39: Esther Shatavsky; 40: (top) Leonard Crosby/The Detroit Public School System, (bottom) Mug Shots/The Stock Market; 41: (top and bottom) Leonard Crosby/The Detroit Public School System; 42: (top) Jose L. Palaez/The Stock Market, (bottom) Leonard Crosby/The Detroit Public School System; 43: Blair Seitz/Photo Researchers, Inc.; 46–47: Stephen Ogilvy; 52: (left) Gordon Alexander, (right) Western History collections, University of Oklahoma Libraries; 53: (top inset) Corbis/Minnesota Historical Society, (bottom inset) George Kerrigan/Impress Graphic Technologies; 54–55: (all photographs) Gordon Alexander; 58: (top inset) Lawrence Migdale/Stock Boston, (bottom inset) Corbis/Charles & Josette Lenars; 58–59: (background) David Sutherland/Tony Stone Images; 61: Corbis/Bettmann; 64: (background) Corbis/Bettmann, (inset) The Charleston Museum; 65: (left and right) Culver Pictures; 66: Courtesy, Library of Congress; 67: From the Collections of Henry Ford Museum and Greenfield Village; 68: (background) Gordon Alexander, (inset) Culver Pictures; 69: Ariel Skelley/The Stock Market; 72–73, Courtesy, Western Reserve Historical Society